NUTS
ABOUT

RECIPES COMPILED BY
EDNA TRULL

McClanahan
Publishing House

Compiled by Edna Trull
Cover and Layout Design: James Asher Graphics
Manufactured in the United States of America

To order call toll free **1-800-544-6959** with Visa or
MasterCard or write:

McClanahan Publishing House, Inc.
P.O. Box 100
Kuttawa, KY 42055

TABLE OF CONTENTS

INTRODUCTION

The pecan, a distinctively delightful nut, is often a key ingredient in festive dishes served at memorable gatherings for good friends and family. It's appearance, whether in a recipe or served alone, signifies "something special."

In this little gift book, we offer you "something special," our favorite recipes from appetizers and entrees to deliciously sinful desserts— all using pecans.

Taste the dishes, share the recipes and savour your success!

APPETIZERS

CORNED BEEF CHEESE BALL

8 ounces cream cheese
1 small package
  corned beef
2 teaspoons
  minced onion

2 to 3 dashes
  garlic powder
Chopped pecans

Soften cream cheese; finely cut corned beef and add to cream cheese. Add other ingredients and roll in a ball or log. Refrigerate to set. Before serving, roll in chopped pecans.

CHEESE BALL

8 ounces cream cheese
4 ounces
  Roquefort cheese
  (or blue cheese)

1 jar Kraft
  Old English cheese
1 small onion, minced
Finely chopped pecans

Have all cheeses at room temperature; mix together well. Add minced onion; shape into ball or small bowl. Top with pecans.

*T*homas Jefferson introduced pecan trees to the east coast from the South. Food historian Waverley Root noted in 1980 that three trees given to George Washington, by Jefferson in 1775, were still growing at Mount Vernon.

DIFFERENT CHEESE RING

1 pound sharp cheddar
  cheese, grated
1 cup chopped pecans
¾ cup mayonnaise
1 medium onion,
  grated

1 clove garlic, pressed
½ teaspoon
  Tabasco sauce
1 cup
  strawberry preserves

Combine all ingredients except preserves. Mix well. Chill and mold into a ring. Chill again. When ready to serve, fill center with preserves. Serve with crackers.

NORTHWEST SALMON BALL

1 large can red salmon
8 ounces cream cheese,
   softened
1 tablespoon
   lemon juice
1 teaspoon dried onion

1 teaspoon horseradish
¼ teaspoon salt
¼ teaspoon
   liquid smoke
Chopped pecans

Drain salmon and mix all ingredients except pecans until well blended. Refrigerate. When ready to serve, shape into ball and roll in pecans. Serve with crackers.

SHRIMP BALL

8 ounces cream cheese, softened	1 tablespoon horseradish
6 ounces tiny shrimp (drain well)	1 tablespoon mayonnaise
¼ cup minced onion	Chopped pecans

Mix all ingredients except pecans by hand and shape into a ball or log. Refrigerate overnight. Before serving, roll in pecan pieces. This recipe doubles well.

*P*ecan production in Georgia is about equal to that of all the other states combined, and two southwest Georgia communites— Albany and Baconton—hold annual fall festivals in celebration of the nut (so does Colfax, a small town in northern Louisiana).

CHEESE PENNIES

½ cup margarine
8 ounces sharp
Cheddar cheese,
  grated

1 cup flour
½ teaspoon salt
½ package dry
  onion soup mix

Soften butter and cheese to room temperature; mix thoroughly. Add dry ingredients and mix well. Shape into a roll and slice. Place 1 whole pecan on top of each and bake at 400° for 8 to 10 minutes. Makes 5 dozen.

HOT CHEESY BEEF DIP

⅓ cup chopped pecans
1½ tablespoons
  melted butter
  or margarine
2-ounce jar dried beef
8 ounces cream cheese,
  softened
2 tablespoons milk

¼ cup finely chopped
  green pepper
¼ cup finely chopped
  green onion
1 clove garlic, pressed
½ teaspoon
  white pepper
½ cup commercial
  sour cream

Sauté pecans in butter 3 to 5 minutes. Drain on paper towels and set aside. Chop dried beef in blender or food processor; set aside. Beat cream cheese and milk with electric mixer on medium speed until smooth. Stir in beef, green pepper, onion, garlic and white pepper, mixing well. Stir in sour cream; spoon into a greased 1-quart casserole. Sprinkle pecans on top; bake at 350° for 25 minutes. Serve dip hot with assorted crackers. Yield: 2 cups.

HOT HAM SPIRALS

1 recipe biscuit dough, prepared
2 cans deviled ham
2 teaspoons mayonnaise
Dash Worcestershire sauce
½ teaspoon seasoned salt
Pinch garlic salt
½ cup finely crushed pecans

Roll biscuit dough out until thin. Combine ham, mayonnaise, seasonings and pecans. Spread onto biscuit dough. Roll into a small roll about the size of a half-dollar and wrap in foil. Refrigerate overnight. Slice and bake at 400° for 8 to 10 minutes or until lightly browned.

PECAN-POTATO BALLS

4 medium potatoes
2 egg yolks
1 teaspoon
  chopped parsley
1 tablespoon minced
  green onion

¼ teaspoon
  cayenne pepper
Salt and pepper
½ cup finely
  chopped pecans
Oil for deep frying

Boil, skin, mash and cool potatoes. Add egg yolks, mixing thoroughly. Add parsley, green onion, cayenne, salt and pepper to taste. Chill mixture several hours. Form potatoes into 1 inch balls. Roll in chopped pecans, pressing to coat. Deep fry 1 to 2 minutes, until crisp. Serve immediately.

BREADS

APPLESAUCE MUFFINS

4 cups flour	2 cups applesauce
2 teaspoons soda	2 sticks
1 teaspoon cloves	melted margarine
3 teaspoons cinnamon	2 cups sugar
2 teaspoons allspice	1 teaspoon vanilla
2 eggs	1 cup chopped pecans

Mix together all dry ingredients. Combine remaining ingredients in a separate bowl; add to dry ingredients. Mix well. Fill muffin tins and bake at 425° for 15 to 20 minutes. Muffins will be lightly browned. Yield: 36 regular muffins.

Note: Batter will keep two weeks if refrigerated. Use as desired. Great to take to shut-ins. Cook in mini-muffin tins and bake for 8 to 10 minutes, instead of 15 minutes.

ORANGE BLOSSOM MUFFINS

12 ounces frozen
   orange juice
   concentrate, thawed
½ cup sugar
4 tablespoons oil
2 eggs, beaten

4 cups biscuit mix
1 cup
   orange marmalade
1 cup chopped,
   toasted pecans

Combine juice, sugar, oil and eggs. Add biscuit mix, marmalade and nuts. Bake at 400° for 20 minutes.

*T*he name pecan is found in several American Indian languages, indicating that the nut was common in the 17th century, but little note was made of it in the first 150 years of European settlement.

PECAN LOAF

2 cups flour
4 teaspoons
   baking powder
1 teaspoon salt
5 tablespoons
   margarine

1 egg, beaten
1 cup milk
½ cup chopped pecans
2 teaspoons sugar,
   optional

Mix and sift flour, baking powder and salt. Cut in margarine or other shortening. Add beaten egg and milk. Stir in pecans; add sugar, if desired. Turn into a buttered 10-inch loaf pan. Let stand 20 minutes. Bake at 350° for 50 minutes.

PUMPKIN-PECAN-RAISIN BREAD

3 cups flour
2 teaspoons
  baking powder
1½ teaspoons salt
1 teaspoon
  baking soda
1 teaspoon cinnamon
½ teaspoon nutmeg
2 eggs

16 ounces canned
  pumpkin
1 cup packed light
  brown sugar
½ cup maple syrup
¼ cup cooking oil
½ cup raisins
½ cup chopped pecans

Mix first 6 ingredients in a large bowl. In a separate bowl, combine the next 5 ingredients. Grease a 9 x 5 inch loaf pan. Stir liquid ingredients into dry ingredients until moistened. Add raisins and pecans, then spoon into loaf pan. Bake at 350° for 1 hour 15 minutes. Cool on wire rack 10 minutes; remove from pan and cool completely on wire rack.

NUT BREAD DELUXE

1 egg
1 cup sugar
1 teaspoon salt
4 teaspoons
  baking powder

4 cups flour,
  sifted twice
1½ cups milk
1 teaspoon melted
  butter or shortening
1 cup chopped pecans

Mix egg and sugar in large bowl. Sift salt, baking powder and flour together. Add to sugar and egg mixture alternately with milk. Stir in melted butter and pecans. Batter should be the consistency of stiff cake batter. Let rise for 30 minutes. Bake at 300° for 2 hours.

BANANA BREAD

½ cup butter	2 cups flour
1 cup sugar	½ teaspoon salt
2 eggs	1 teaspoon vanilla
1 teaspoon soda	3 bananas, mashed
1 tablespoon water	½ cup pecans

Cream butter and sugar; add eggs and beat. Dissolve soda in water; add to egg mixture. Mix in flour and salt. Add vanilla, bananas and pecans. Pour into greased and floured deep loaf pan and bake at 350° for 1 hour. Test for doneness. Makes 1 large loaf.

DATE AND CHEESE NUT BREAD

8 ounces
  chopped dates
¾ cup boiling water
1¾ cups flour
¼ teaspoon salt

1 teaspoon soda
½ cup sugar
1 egg, beaten
¾ cup chopped pecans
1 cup grated
  American cheese

Soak dates in boiling water 5 minutes. Sift flour, salt, soda and sugar together. Add egg, nuts and cheese, mixing well. Bake in greased 5 x 9 loaf pan at 350° for 50 minutes.

APRICOT BREAD

1 cup dried apricots, chopped	2 cups flour
1 cup warm water	2 teaspoons baking powder
1 cup sugar	¼ teaspoon baking soda
2 tablespoons margarine, melted	⅛ teaspoon salt
½ cup orange juice concentrate	1 cup chopped pecans

Preheat oven to 325°. Soak apricots in warm water, drain excess water and reserve. Stir in sugar, margarine, ¼ cup reserved juice and orange juice concentrate. Combine flour, baking powder, soda and salt. Add to apricot mixture. Blend in nuts. Let mixture stand for 20 minutes. Bake in greased and floured 9 x 5 x 3 loaf pan for 1 hour and 15 minutes.

STRAWBERRY NUT BREAD

3 cups sifted flour
1 teaspoon
  baking powder
1 teaspoon salt
1 tablespoon cinnamon

1 ¼ cups
  chopped pecans
2 cups sugar
4 eggs, beaten
1 ¼ cups vegetable oil
2 cups frozen sliced
  strawberries, thawed

Sift together all dry ingredients in a large bowl. Combine remaining ingredients, mixing well. Make a well in center of dry ingredients; add liquid to moisten dry ingredients. Pour into 2 greased 9 x 5 x 3 loaf pans. Bake at 350° for 1 hour. Let cool 5 minutes, then enjoy.

SOUP

&

SALADS

SOUTHERN CREAM OF PECAN SOUP

2 tablespoons butter
3 tablespoons finely
  chopped onion
1 tablespoon
  all-purpose flour
2 cups chicken stock
  or broth
½ teaspoon salt

Freshly ground pepper
1 cup finely
  ground pecans
1 small sprig
  celery leaves
1½ cups light cream
  or half-and-half
4 small sprigs mint

Melt butter in heavy saucepan over medium heat.
Add onion and sauté. Stir in flour; cook, stirring,
over low heat 1 minute. Gradually pour in stock,
stirring constantly. Stir in salt and pepper to taste.
Add pecans and sprig of celery leaves. Increase
heat to medium; heat soup to boiling. Reduce heat
to low. Simmer 10 minutes, stirring occasionally.
Stir in cream; simmer over very low heat 5 minutes.
Ladle into individual warmed bowls. Top with a
sprig of mint. Serve at once. Serves 4.

FROZEN STRAWBERRY SALAD

16 ounces frozen
   strawberries
16 ounces
   crushed pineapple

6 ounces softened
   cream cheese
1 pint cream, whipped
1 cup chopped pecans

Cut strawberries in half. Add all other ingredients, stir. Freeze in a 9 x 15 pan. Serves 6 to 10.

*T*he pecan is known botanically as the Illinois hickory, but the tree on which it is grown thrives almost exclusively in a band of the deep South stretching from coastal Georgia to Texas.

FROZEN CRANBERRY SALAD

1 can cranberry sauce
1 cup non-dairy
  whipped topping
1 small can crushed
  pineapple, drained

¼ cup powdered sugar
¼ cup mayonnaise
¾ cup chopped pecans

Mix all ingredients together. Freeze in paper-lined muffin tins. After freezing, salads can be put in a plastic bag and used as needed.

> *T*he discovery of the pecan belongs
> to the American Indian. Long
> before the white man ever set foot on
> American soil, the pecan was considered
> a precious commodity traded for goods
> of equal value. The Indian called this
> naturally delicious hard-shelled nut a
> "pacan" which is an Indian word
> intended to designate all nuts with a shell
> so hard it had to be cracked with a stone.

BARBARA'S RAINBOW SALAD

2 small carrots,
  coarsely grated
2 ribs celery, chopped
¼ head purple
  cabbage, grated
1 Granny Smith apple,
  cored and chopped

3 tablespoons
  chopped pecans
1 tablespoon
  mayonnaise
3 tablespoons
  plain yogurt

Mix all ingredients together and serve. Serves 4 to 6.

SPECIAL DAYS SALAD

15 ounces pineapple tidbits	2 cups whole fresh strawberries
1 can Mandarin oranges	1 cup pecans
1½ cups diced apples	6 ounces sugar-free instant vanilla pudding
¾ cup diced bananas	
1 cup seedless grapes	3 tablespoons Tang

Drain and reserve liquid from pineapple and oranges. Mix fruits and nuts in large bowl and toss. In separate bowl, combine pudding and Tang with juices. Whip to make thick sauce. Pour over fruit and refrigerate overnight. (Whole frozen strawberries can be used, but wait to put them in until just before serving.)

CONGEALED CRANBERRY SALAD

6 ounces lemon gelatin
16 ounces whole berry
  cranberry sauce
2 cups boiling water
8 ounces
  crushed pineapple

½ to 1 cup finely
  chopped celery
¼ to ½ cup
  chopped pecans
Mayonnaise
Nutmeg

Dissolve gelatin and cranberry sauce in boiling water. Drain pineapple, reserving liquid. Add pineapple to gelatin mixture. When gelatin begins to thicken, add celery and nuts. Serve topped with mayonnaise softened with a small amount of reserved pineapple juice. Sprinkle with ground nutmeg. Serves 8.

CRANBERRY SALAD

2 cups whole
   cranberry sauce
2 cup boiling water
6 ounces cherry or
   raspberry gelatin

½ cup cold water
½ cup orange juice
Rind of one orange
¼ cup sugar, optional
1 cup pecans
1 large apple, chopped

Soften cranberry sauce in boiling water. Add remaining ingredients and refrigerate to set. Stir once after partially set.

This makes a large salad.

GRAPEFRUIT PINEAPPLE SALAD

3 ounces lemon gelatin
1 cup hot ginger ale
Pinch salt
1 tablespoon vinegar

1 tablespoon sugar
2 grapefruit, sectioned
1 small can crushed
   pineapple, undrained
Toasted pecans

Add gelatin to hot giner ale, stirring until completely dissolved. Chill slightly and add remaining ingredients. Pour into ring mold that has been lightly coated with mayonnaise. Refrigerate until congealed.

Chopped maraschino cherries may be added for color if desired. Serves 6.

From *Cooking with Curtis Grace*; used by permission.

APRICOT SALAD

6 ounces
  apricot gelatin
15 ounces crushed
  pineapple, drained,
  reserving juice

8 ounces non-dairy
  whipped topping
2 cups buttermilk
1 cup chopped pecans

Dissolve gelatin in heated pineapple juice. Let cool. Add remaining ingredients, mixing well. Refrigerate.

FROZEN FRUIT SALAD

15 ounces crushed
   pineapple, drained
1 banana, chopped
10 maraschino
   cherries, quartered

½ cup chopped pecans
½ cup sugar
1 tablespoon
   lemon juice
1 small carton
   sour cream

Mix all ingredients and freeze in gelatin mold.

The pecan is the second most popular member of the nut family. Peanuts are the most popular.

PRETZEL SALAD

First layer:
2 cups crushed pretzels

¾ cup margarine, melted
3 tablespoons sugar

Second layer:
8 ounces cream cheese

1 cup sugar
4½ ounces non-dairy whipped topping

Third layer:
6 ounces strawberry gelatin

2 cups boiling water
20 ounces frozen sweetened strawberries

Mix first layer and put in 9 x 13 pan. Heat in 400° oven for 5 minutes. Cool. Mix second layer and add to first; mix and add third layer. Refrigerate.

CHERRY PECAN SALAD

1 can cherry pie filling	1 large container non-dairy whipped topping
1 large can crushed pineapple, drained	
1 cup pecans	1 can sweetened condensed milk

Combine all ingredients and refrigerate before serving.

FRUIT SALAD WITH HONEY DRESSING

1 cup
  grapefruit sections
1 cup sliced bananas
1 cup sliced peaches

1 cup orange sections
1 cup
  pineapple chunks
1 cup chopped pecans

Dressing:
8 ounces softened
  cream cheese
Juice of 1 lemon

¼ cup honey
1 cup whipping cream

Drain fruits, add nuts and chill. Blend cream cheese with honey and lemon juice until smooth. Whip cream until soft peaks form. Fold into cream cheese mixture. Serve over fruit, garnish with mint leaves.

CONGEALED LEMON AND
PIMENTO CHEESE SALAD

3 ounces lemon gelatin
1 cup boiling water
½ cup sugar
1 small jar pimiento
  cheese spread

1 small can crushed
  pineapple, drained
9 ounces Cool Whip
1 cup toasted pecans

Dissolve gelatin in boiling water. Add sugar and cheese spread. Mix well. Add drained pineapple. Let congeal to consistency of unbeaten egg whites. Fold in Cool Whip and pecans. Pour into oiled ring mold. Refrigerate to congeal. Serves 6 to 8.

From *Cooking with Curtis Grace*. Used by permission.

CRAN-APPLESALAD

6 ounces cherry gelatin
2 cups boiling water
1½ cups chilled
  pineapple juice

1 can whole
  cranberry sauce
1 cup chopped celery
1 cup chopped pecans
1 cup chopped apples

Dissolve gelatin in boiling water. Add juice. Chill until partially set. Add remaining ingredients. Refrigerate.

*G*eorgia traces the pecan industry to 1840, when a ship captain named Samuel Flood is said to have found pecans floating at sea and planted them at his home port of St. Marys, in the southeast corner of the state.

"AUBURN" BROCCOLI SALAD

1 bunch broccoli
1 bunch spring onions
½ cup golden raisins

6 slices crisp bacon,
    crumbled
½ cup pecans

Dressing:
1 cup salad dressing

½ cup sugar
2 tablespoons vinegar

Soak broccoli in salted water for 30 minutes. Cut into bite-sized pieces. Slice onions. Combine broccoli, onions and raisins. One hour before serving, combine dressing ingredients and pour over broccoli, raisins and onions. Keep refrigerated. Add bacon pieces and pecans just before serving.

MOLDED CABBAGE SALAD

3 ounces lime gelatin
1 cup hot water
1 cup miniature
   marshmallows
1 cup crushed
   pineapple, drained
⅔ cup pineapple juice

1 cup mayonnaise
1½ cups
   shredded cabbage
½ can pimiento
2 cups
   whipped topping
1 cup chopped pecans

Dissolve gelatin in hot water, add marshmallows
and stir until melted. Add pineapple, pineapple
juice, mayonnaise, cabbage and pimiento. Let
stand until mixture begins to thicken. Add whipped topping and pecans. Turn into mold which
has been coated lightly with mayonnaise.
Refrigerate until set. Unmold onto plate of lettuce
leaves and garnish with radishes, grapes, parsley,
etc.

Note: any flavor gelatin may be substituted for
lime.

CHICKEN SALAD

1 chicken, cooked
  and boned
8 ounces sour cream
½ cup salad dressing

1 cup chopped celery
1 cup chopped pecans
6 pieces crisp bacon,
  crumbled
1 lemon

Mix all ingredients together and squeeze lemon juice into mixture. Mix well and serve on lettuce or sandwiches.

FRUITED TURKEY SALAD

4 cups cubed
   cooked turkey
1½ cups seedless
   green grapes, halved
1½ cups small
   cantaloupe balls

1 cup chopped celery
3 to 4 tablespoons
   lemon juice
½ teaspoon salt
¾ cup mayonnaise
   or salad dressing
¾ cup pecans

Combine turkey, grapes, cantaloupe and celery.
In a small bowl, combine juice, salt and
mayonnaise. Pour over turkey and mix well.
Chill at least one hour. Add pecans just before
serving. Serve on lettuce.

CASSEROLES, VEGETABLES & SIDE DISHES

BAKED CRANBERRY RELISH

1 quart raw
   cranberries, washed

1½ cups sugar
1 teaspoon cinnamon
½ cup pecans

Preheat oven to 275°. Combine berries with sugar in an ungreased 1½-quart deep-dish baking dish. Bake, uncovered, for 1 hour or until berries become juicy. Increase oven temperature to 350°. Sprinkle cinnamon over top of berries, cover and bake for 15 minutes, or just until berries are clear but still whole. Sprinkle pecans on top and serve warm with roast turkey or roast pork. This will keep refrigerated for 1 week.

PINEAPPLE CASSEROLE

1 stick margarine	½ cup flour
40-ounces pineapple chunks, drained	1 stack Ritz crackers
1 cup sugar	½ cup chopped pecans

Dot bottom of dish with ½ of margarine. Mix pineapple, sugar and flour. Pour in dish; cover with Ritz crackers. Dot with rest of margarine and sprinkle pecans on top. Bake at 350° for 20 to 25 minutes.

BROCCOLI-PECAN CASSEROLE

2 packages
frozen broccoli
1 can cream of
mushroom soup
1 cup mayonnaise
¾ cup chopped pecans

2 eggs, well beaten
1 medium onion,
chopped
1 cup grated
sharp cheese
2 cups buttered
bread crumbs

Cook broccoli. Drain. Add soup, mayonnaise and pecans. Mix. Add eggs and onions. Pour into casserole, top with cheese and buttered crumbs. Bake at 350° for 30 minutes.

CABBAGE CASSEROLE

1 medium cabbage, chopped

10 ounces cream of celery soup

8 ounces sliced water chestnuts

½ cup salad dressing

½ cup toasted pecans

8 ounces Stove Top Stuffing mix

¾ cup grated Cheddar cheese

Boil cabbage until tender. Drain. Mix soup, water chestnuts and salad dressing with drained cabbage. Place in a buttered casserole. Top with pecans which have been mixed with stuffing mix. Sprinkle with cheese. Bake at 350° until bubbly.

SWEET POTATO CASSEROLE

3 cups mashed
   sweet potatoes
1 cup sugar*
2 eggs, beaten
1 cup coconut
½ cup milk
¾ stick margarine,
   melted

1 teaspoon vanilla
1 cup
   light brown sugar
½ cup flour
¾ stick margarine,
   softened
1 cup chopped pecans

Mix first 7 ingredients and pour in casserole dish. Combine remaining ingredients and sprinkle on top. Bake at 350° for 30 minutes or until browned.

*A mixture of ½ cup granulated sugar and ½ cup brown sugar may be used if desired.

SUMMER SQUASH CASSEROLE

2 tablespoons butter
¼ cup
  buttery flavored
  cracker crumbs
¼ cup chopped pecans
¼ cup water
½ teaspoon salt
1 pound
  yellow squash, sliced

¼ cup mayonnaise
1 egg, beaten
½ cup shredded
  Cheddar cheese
2 tablespoons butter,
  melted
1½ teaspoons sugar
¼ to ½ teaspoon
  instant minced onion

Microwave butter in a 1-quart casserole until melted. Add crumbs and pecans; microwave 2 minutes, stirring after 1 minute. Pour crumbs onto wax paper and set aside. Place water, salt and squash in same dish. Cover and microwave 8 to 10 minutes, stirring after 4 minutes, until squash is tender. Drain. Combine remaining ingredients. Pour over squash, mixing well. Microwave at medium power 2 to 4 minutes more, until center is set. Let stand 5 minutes before serving. Serves 4.

PECAN-BROWN RICE PILAF

½ cup chopped
  green onions
1 tablespoon
  vegetable oil
2½ cups water
1½ teaspoons
  chicken-flavored
  bouillon granules

½ teaspoon
  dried thyme
⅛ teaspoon pepper
1 cup brown rice,
  uncooked
¼ cup chopped
  pecans, toasted
2 tablespoons
  chopped parsley

Sauté onions in oil until tender. Add water and next 3 ingredients; bring to a boil. Remove from heat and add rice. Stir. Transfer rice to a 1½-quart baking dish. Cover and bake at 350° for 50 minutes. Stir in pecans and chopped parsley. Serves 6.

CRAN-APPLE CASSEROLE

2 cups
  fresh cranberries
3 cups apples,
  peeled and chopped
1 cup sugar

½ cup margarine
1 cup
  quick-cooking oats
1 cup brown sugar

Mix berries, apples and sugar; place in baking dish. Melt margarine, add oats and brown sugar; pour over fruit mixture. Bake at 350° for 1 hour. Serves 8.

The pecan—a native American nut—is hardly grown or eaten at all outside the United States.

PECAN YAMS WITH MARSHMALLOWS

2 pounds yams,
  about 6
½ cup coarsely
  chopped pecans

½ cup sugar
2 tablespoons butter
  or margarine
1 cup marshmallows

Peel yams, slice lengthwise in ¼-inch thick slices.
Put in buttered baking dish. Sprinkle pecans
and sugar over yams. Dot with butter. Bake at
375° for 45 minutes, or until yams are tender. Top
with marshmallows. Return to oven until
marshmallows are melted. Serves 6.

BO'S SWEET POTATOES
IN ORANGE SHELLS

5 large sweet potatoes,
  boiled
1 stick butter
½ cup orange juice
¼ cup sherry

¼ teaspoon finely
  grated orange rind
Salt and pepper
  to taste
Chopped pecans
Pecan halves

Skin and mash sweet potatoes; add butter, orange juice and sherry in small amounts at a time so as not to make the potatoes juicy. Add orange zest, salt and pepper. Fill orange shells with potato mixture. Sprinkle with pecans and top with pecan half. Place in 350° oven to heat before serving.

BAKED NUTS 'N' BERRIES DRESSING

1 pan (9 x 9 x 2")
cornbread, cooled
and crumbled
6 cups white
bread cubes
1 cup Sunnyland
Pecan Pieces

1 teaspoon
poultry seasoning
16 ounces whole berry
cranberry sauce
½ cup butter or
margarine, melted
1 egg, beaten lightly

Combine cornbread, bread cubes, nuts and poultry seasoning. Stir in cranberry sauce, butter and egg; toss lightly. Bake in 3-quart casserole at 350° for 45 minutes. Makes 2½ quarts dressing.

ENTRÉES

VEGETABLE STIR-FRY

Celery
Onion
Broccoli
Carrots
Water Chestnuts
Red Pepper
Chinese pea pods
Mushrooms
Bamboo shoots

2 tablespoons oil
Chicken breasts,
   uncooked
Salt and pepper
Soy sauce, optional
Cooked rice
Pecans,
   chopped or whole

Chop, shred, or dice vegetables according to your preference. Slice or dice chicken breasts. Heat oil in wok or electric skillet and sauté chicken until no longer pink. Add vegetables and stir. Season to taste with salt and pepper. Add soy sauce if desired, and stir constantly until chicken is thoroughly cooked and vegetables are crisp-tender. Serve over cooked rice and sprinkle pecans on top.

Note: quantities are not given for vegetables due to individual preference.

CHICKEN IN SOUR CREAM

8 whole boned
 breasts of chicken
Salt and pepper
White wine
1 pint sour cream

Butter
¼ cup chopped pecans
Paprika
2 tablespoons sherry

Season chicken with salt and pepper. Wash liberally with white wine and sour cream. Cover and refrigerate at least 2 hours. Remove from marinade and scrape mixture from each piece. Brush with butter. Brown in skillet 10 minutes. Transfer to baking dish and add pecans to marinade. Mix well. Pour over chicken. Bake at 300° until tender. Add paprika. Pour sherry into pockets between breasts.

CHICKEN WITH PEARS & STUFFING

2 tablespoons oil
6 boneless chicken
  breast halves
¼ teaspoon
  garlic powder
¼ teaspoon salt
¼ teaspoon pepper
1¾ cups apple juice
6 ounces chicken
  flavor stuffing mix
2 pears, cored and
  sliced ¼-inch thick
¼ cup pecans

Heat oil in large skillet and lightly brown chicken on both sides. Sprinkle with garlic powder, salt and pepper. Pour in apple juice and bring to boil. Reduce heat and simmer for 5 to 10 minutes. Stir in contents of vegetable/seasoning packet from stuffing mix. Add sliced pears and simmer 5 minutes longer.

Place chicken on serving platter—keep warm. Stir stuffing crumbs and pecans into skillet. Mix well. Cover, let stand 5 minutes, and serve.

CHICKEN CRUNCH

10 ounces cream of
  mushroom soup
½ cup milk
1 teaspoon
  parsley flakes
1 teaspoon
  minced onion

8 boneless
  chicken breasts
1 package stuffing mix
½ cup toasted pecans
2 tablespoons butter,
  melted

Mix soup, milk, parsley flakes and onion. Dip
chicken breasts in soup mixture, then roll in stuffing mix and pecans. Shape like a potato; put in
a baking dish. Pour butter over. Bake at 350° for
1 hour. Cover with foil to prevent browning too
quickly.

CRANBERRY PECAN CHICKEN

12 ounces cranberries	16 ounces butter
8 ounces orange juice	or margarine,
8 ounces sugar	room temperature
4 ounces pecans,	2 chicken breasts
finely chopped	

Combine cranberries, orange juice and sugar in saucepan. Bring to a boil and simmer 20 minutes or until cranberries are soft. Remove from heat and cool to room temperature. Purée cranberries in food processor just until blended. Add softened butter and process until smooth and thoroughly mixed. Remove and fold in chopped pecans. Drop by spoonfuls onto waxed paper and freeze. When frozen, transfer to freezer container. Bone, skin and lightly season chicken breasts. Grill on hot grill, turning over when outside edges turn white. Cook completely. Place 2 pieces of cranberry mixture on top of each cooked chicken breast and soften. Makes 2 servings.

From *Lake Superior's NORTH SHORE in Good Taste*, Bluefin Bay Resort. Used by permission.

DREAM CHICKEN

1 large chicken, cooked	1 cup pecans
2 envelopes	1 cup canned peas
unflavored gelatin	2 cups diced celery
2 cups stock	3 hard-boiled eggs
1 cup mayonnaise	½ cup pimiento

Cook chicken, reserving stock. Skin chicken and remove from bones. Dissolve gelatin in heated stock. Cool. Combine all ingredients and place in molds or bowl and refrigerate. Serve on lettuce leaves.

HOT CHICKEN SALAD

3 cups cooked chicken
1 cup mayonnaise
2 cups finely
 chopped celery
2 tablespoons
 grated onion
½ cup chopped
 pecans, toasted

½ teaspoon salt
1 teaspoon
 monosodium
 glutamate
1 teaspoon tarragon
1 cup crushed
 potato chips
½ cup grated cheese

Mix first 8 ingredients well and turn into greased baking dish. Top with potato chips and cheese which have been combined. Bake at 450° for 10 minutes and serve immediately. Serves 8 to 10.

*G*eorge Washington was very
fond of pecans. He carried
them in his pockets all through the
Revolutionary War.

PECAN DIJON CHICKEN

4 chicken breast halves, skinned and boned	¼ cup Dijon mustard
¼ cup honey	1 cup finely chopped pecans

Place each piece of chicken between 2 sheets of waxed paper; flatten to ¼ inch thickness using a meat mallet or rolling pin. Set aside. Combine honey and mustard; spread on both sides of chicken; dredge chicken in chopped pecans. Arrange chicken in a lightly greased shallow baking dish. Bake at 350° for 30 minutes or until tender. Serves 4.

BAKED CHICKEN WITH PECANS

1 large onion
1 clove garlic
½ bell pepper
½ cup flour
1 tablespoon paprika
½ cup butter or
  margarine, melted
6 chicken breasts
1 cup fresh tomatoes,
  quartered
¼ cup fresh parsley or
  2 tablespoons dried
1 tablespoon
  Worcestershire sauce

1 teaspoon
  curry powder
1 teaspoon thyme
2 tablespoons vinegar
2 tablespoons
  dry mustard
1 cup currants or
  white raisins
1 cup fresh
  mushrooms or
  4½ ounces canned
½ cup large
  pecan pieces

Preheat oven to 300°. Chop and sauté onion, garlic and bell pepper; set aside. Mix together flour and paprika. Dip chicken breasts in melted butter; roll in flour. Brown and place in 3½ quart casserole. Top with sautéed vegetables, tomatoes and parsley. Mix Worcestershire sauce, curry, thyme, vinegar and mustard together and pour over chicken. Bake for 40 minutes. Remove from oven and add currants, mushrooms and pecans. Bake an additional 15 minutes and serve.

STUFFED GREEN PEPPERS

4 medium-sized
  green peppers
2 tablespoons
  shortening
1½ pounds
  ground beef
1 tablespoon
  minced onion
2 tablespoons finely
  chopped celery

1 cup cooked rice
1 cup Sunnyland
  Pecan Pieces
1 teaspoon salt
1 cup tomato juice,
  divided
½ cup grated
  Cheddar cheese

Wash peppers; remove stems and seeds. Cover with boiling salted water; cook 10 minutes. Drain. Melt shortening in frying pan; add meat, onion and celery. Sauté until meat is browned and celery soft. Combine thoroughly with rice, pecans, salt and ½ cup tomato juice. Fill pepper and sprinkle cheese over tops. Place in greased baking pan; pour remaining juice around peppers. Bake at 350° for 30 minutes or until cheese is golden-brown. Serves 4.

CRAB CASSEROLE

2 cups crab meat
2 cups finely
  chopped celery
1 cup mayonnaise
½ cup pecans
1 cup toasted
  bread crumbs

½ teaspoon salt
2 tablespoons
  lemon juice
1 teaspoon
  grated onion
Crushed potato chips
½ cup grated cheese

Mix first 8 ingredients together. Place in baking dish. Top with crushed potato chips and cheese. Bake at 425° for 10 to 15 minutes.

ESCALLOPED FISH WITH PECANS

1 cup flaked
   cooked fish
2 cups medium
   white sauce
1 cup Sunnyland
   Pecan Pieces

2 hard-cooked eggs,
   minced
Cracker crumbs
Butter

Combine fish, white sauce, nuts and eggs. Pour into greased casserole, cover with crumbs and dot with butter. Bake at 350° for 25 minutes. Serves 4.

*P*ecans are a rich source of Vitamin B-6. Most foods containing B-6 (soybeans, wheat, etc.,) are cooked before eaten. Cooking destroys B-6. Pecans are delicious raw.

ORANGE ROUGHY with PECANS AND BROWN BUTTER SAUCE

6 orange roughy filets
Seasoning mix*
½ cup milk
1 egg yolk
1 cup flour

Vegetable oil
Brown Butter Sauce**
Pecan-Butter Sauce***
½ cup chopped pecans

Sprinkle fish with 1 ½ tablespoons seasoning mix; set aside. Combine milk and egg yolk. Combine flour and remaining seasoning mix; dredge fish in flour; dip in milk; dredge again in flour. Heat 1 inch of oil in electric skillet to 350°. Fry 2 to 3 minutes on each side. Drain well and keep warm. Spoon Brown Butter Sauce onto platter. Place fish on sauce and spread each filet with 3 tablespoons Pecan-Butter Sauce. Sprinkle with ½ cup pecans. Serve immediately.

*Seasoning Mix
2 tablespoons
  Greek seasoning
1 teaspoon
  onion powder
1 teaspoon paprika

1 teaspoon Creole
  seasoning mix
½ teaspoon red pepper
½ teaspoon
  black pepper
½ teaspoon
  white pepper

Combine all ingredients in a small bowl, mixing well.

**Brown Butter Sauce
1 cup chicken broth
1 teaspoon
   minced garlic
½ cup butter, divided

2 tablespoons flour
¼ cup Worcestershire
   sauce
½ teaspoon hot sauce

Combine broth and garlic in a small saucepan. Bring to a boil. Reduce heat and simmer 2 to 3 minutes. Melt ¼ cup butter in a heavy saucepan over low heat. Add flour, stirring until smooth. Cook 1 minute, stirring constantly. Gradually add broth mixture, stirring constantly. Add remaining butter, Worcestershire sauce and hot sauce. Cook over medium heat, stirring, until mixture is thickened and bubbly.

***Pecan-Butter Sauce
½ cup butter, melted
1 cup chopped pecans
2 tablespoons
   chopped onions

½ teaspoons
   minced garlic
1 tablespoon
   lemon juice
1 teaspoon hot sauce

Combine all ingredients in container of food processor and cover with lid. Process until smooth.

PORK CHOPS
WITH PECAN CREAM SAUCE

3 tablespoons vegetable oil	4 center-cut loin pork chops, cut ¾-inch thick
2 tablespoons butter	½ cup dry white wine
¾ cup finely chopped onion	Salt & pepper to taste
3 ounces fresh mushrooms, cut into slices	½ cup heavy cream
	⅓ cup coarsely chopped pecans
	3 tablespoons finely chopped parsley

Heat oil and butter in large skillet. Add onion and sauté. Add mushrooms and sauté. Remove onion and mushrooms from skillet with slotted spoon; reserve. Add pork chops to skillet. Cook until brown on both sides. Spoon off as much fat as possible. Set skillet over low heat. Add reserved onion and mushrooms, wine and salt and pepper. Simmer, covered 10 to 12 minutes. Stir cream, pecans and parsley into sauce mixture; increase heat to medium high. Cook, uncovered, until sauce thickens, about 10 minutes. Transfer chops to serving platter. Pour sauce over chops and serve immediately.

CANDIES
&
COOKIES

CARAMELIZED PECANS

⅓ cup syrup or honey Pinch salt
1½ cups brown sugar 1 tablespoon
½ cup water   melted butter
      3 cups toasted pecans

Combine syrup, sugar, water and salt. Cook until soft ball stage. Remove from heat, add butter and beat until thick. Stir in pecans and coat each piece. Separate while warm.

To toast pecans: place whole pecan halves in large shallow pan with one stick melted margarine. Bake at 250°, stirring every 15 minutes until toasted (approximately 1 to 1½ hours). Salt while hot.

EASY PECAN BRITTLE

2 cups pecans
2 cups sugar
¼ teaspoon salt

¼ teaspoon
baking soda
1 teaspoon vanilla

Spread pecans close together in shallow 9 x 9 buttered pan. Melt sugar slowly in iron skillet until light and golden colored. Remove from heat; stir in salt, soda and vanilla. Pour over pecans. Break into pieces when cold.

*P*ecans are perishable and require cool, dry storage. They keep well in a tightly-sealed package in the refrigerator. For extended storage, freezing is best.

PRALINES

1 package butterscotch pudding, not instant	½ cup evaporated milk
1 cup granulated sugar	1 tablespoon butter
½ cup brown sugar	1 ½ cups broken pecans

Cook and stir pudding, sugars, milk and butter over low heat in a heavy saucepan until sugars dissolve. Add pecans and bring to a full boil. Boil slowly for 3 to 5 minutes, stirring often until soft ball stage. Remove from heat and beat until candy thickens but still looks shiny. Drop quickly with tablespoon onto waxed paper to form 2-inch patties. Makes 24 candies.

PECAN CARAMELS

14 ounces caramels	Margarine
4 tablespoons milk	½ bar paraffin
2 cups pecan pieces	12 ounces semi-sweet chocolate morsels

Melt caramels in milk over low heat; add pecans. Drop by teaspoonfuls onto buttered waxed paper. Chill. Melt paraffin and chocolate pieces in saucepan over low heat. Dip caramels into chocolate. Return to waxed paper. Chill.

CARAMEL PECAN KISSES

9 caramel candies   36 pecan halves
9 chocolate kisses

Line an 8 x 8 x 2 inch microwave-safe baking dish
with a sheet of waxed paper. Remove wrappers
from caramels and kisses. Evenly space caramels
on microwave cooking paper. Microwave on
high until caramels are softened, 30 seconds.
Flatten by pressing 4 pecan halves into each
caramel. Top each caramel with a chocolate kiss.
Microwave on high 15 seconds longer. Let stand
1 minute. Gently press chocolate kisses to attach
to caramels. Refrigerate until set. Remove candies
from waxed paper. Cover and store at room
temperature. Makes 9 candies.

RUM BALLS

1 cup ground pecans	3 tablespoons
1 cup ground	white corn syrup
vanilla wafers	6 tablespoons rum
3 tablespoons cocoa	Powdered sugar

Mix first 3 ingredients. Add syrup and rum; mix well. Form into balls about 1 inch in diameter. Roll in powdered sugar. Store in cookie tins. Makes about 50.

COCONUT KISSES

2 egg whites
⅔ cup sugar
½ teaspoon vanilla
2 cups
  corn flakes cereal

3½ ounces
  flaked coconut
½ cup chopped pecans

Preheat oven to 350°. Beat egg whites (at room temperature) at high speed of electric mixer until foamy. Gradually add sugar, 1 tablespoon at a time, beating until stiff peaks form. Fold in vanilla, cereal, coconut and pecans. Drop by teaspoonfuls onto cookie sheets lined with aluminum foil. Place in oven and immediately turn off heat. Do not open oven for 8 hours. Carefully peel cookies from foil. Yield: 3 dozen.

CHUNKY NUT CLUSTERS

16 ounces almond bark
3 squares unsweetened
   chocolate

12 ounces
   chocolate chips
12 ounces pecans,
   chopped
1½ cups raisins

Melt almond bark and chocolate in heavy pan over low heat. Add nuts and raisins; mix well. Drop by teaspoonfuls on waxed paper. Freeze to set.

A 5-pound package of unshelled pecans may contain more than 3 pounds or less than one pound of kernels, depending on the variety and the quality. Good grade unshelled pecans average about 50% kernel.

APPLESAUCE DELIGHTS

1 ½ cups flour
1 teaspoon salt
1 teaspoon
 baking soda
1 cup quick-cooking
 oats
½ cup non-fat
 dry milk
¾ cup brown sugar
1 teaspoon cinnamon

2 dashes allspice
½ cup raisins
½ cup chopped pecans
1 teaspoon
 egg replacer
1 tablespoon water
½ cup
 melted margarine
2 teaspoons vinegar
1 cup applesauce

Combine first 8 ingredients; add raisins and pecans. Mix egg replacer and water, add to mixture. Stir in margarine, vinegar and applesauce; blend well. Spread in greased 9 x 9 or 12 x 8 pan. Bake at 350° for 30 to 35 minutes. Cool and cut into bars.

CRISPY OATMEAL SQUARES

½ cup melted margarine	½ cup chopped pecans
½ cup sugar	½ cup raisins
1½ cups quick-cooking oats	½ teaspoon vanilla

Mix all ingredients together and press into a lightly greased 9 x 9 baking pan. Bake at 375° for 15 minutes. Cool on rack and cut into squares.

FUDGE SCOTCH BARS

2 cups graham
  cracker crumbs
1 can sweetened
  condensed milk

½ cup chocolate chips
½ cup
  butterscotch chips
½ cup chopped pecans

Blend all ingredients. Mix well; press into 9 x 9 pan. Bake at 350° for 30 to 35 minutes. Cool on rack and cut into bars.

*O*ne cup of pecans equals about 3½ ounces, or about 4½ cups per pound.

CHEWY CARAMEL BROWNIES

14 ounces caramels
12 ounces
  evaporated milk
1 box German
  chocolate cake mix

¼ cup melted butter
1 teaspoon vanilla
1 cup chopped pecans
1 cup chocolate chips

Combine caramels and ⅓ cup evaporated milk; cook over low heat until caramels are melted. Remove from heat. Mix cake mix, butter, vanilla, pecans and ⅓ cup evaporated milk into a dough. Press ½ of mixture into a 9 x 13 greased pan. You might need a little more to cover the pan. Bake at 350° for 10 to 12 minutes; remove and cool slightly. Drizzle caramel mixture over the cooked dough and sprinkle chocolate chips on top. Gently spread the rest of the dough over chips. Bake at 350° an additional 20 to 25 minutes. Cool; cut into bars.

MARK'S SHORTBREAD

1 cup butter
½ cup packed
  brown sugar

2½ cups flour
½ cup toasted pecans
½ cup chocolate chips

Cream butter and brown sugar until fluffy. Stir in flour until the dough is not sticky, then mix in pecans. Press into a 9 x 13 x 2 pan. Bake at 300° for 30 minutes, or until golden brown. Remove from oven and spread chocolate chips over top. Place back in oven for a few minutes. Cool on rack and cut into squares.

ICE BOX COOKIES

1 cup butter	3½ cups flour
2 cups brown sugar	½ teaspoon salt
2 eggs	1 teaspoon soda
	1 cup chopped pecans

Cream butter and sugar; add eggs, mix well. Sift flour, salt and soda together. Add nuts and mix all ingredients together. Turn out on floured board and shape into rolls. Wrap in waxed paper. Store in refrigerator overnight. Slice very thin! Bake at 300° to 350° until crisp and lightly browned, 12 to 15 minutes.

NUTTY FINGERS

6 tablespoons
powdered sugar
¾ cup butter, softened
2 cups flour

Pinch salt
1 cup pecans, chopped
1 teaspoon vanilla

Combine sugar, butter, flour, salt and pecans. Add vanilla, and 1 teaspoon ice water, if needed. Mix well and shape in fingers. Bake at 300° about 45 minutes. Roll in powdered sugar.

NINTH STREET HOUSE
PECAN CRISPIES

1 cup margarine
½ cup sugar
1 teaspoon vanilla

½ cup crushed
   potato chips
½ cup chopped pecans
2 cups sifted flour

Cream butter, sugar and vanilla. Add potato chips and pecans. Stir in flour. Roll into small balls. Place on ungreased cookie sheet. Press balls flat with bottom of glass that has been dipped in sugar. Bake at 350° for 16 to 18 minutes, until lightly browned. Yield: 3 dozen cookies.

From *Cook Talk with Curtis Grace and Friends.* Used by permission.

HOLIDAY HUNKS

1 cup softened butter	3 cups flour
1½ cups sugar	1 teaspoon cinnamon
3 eggs	1 teaspoon
1 teaspoon	ground cloves
baking soda	1 pound
2 tablespoons	chopped pecans
hot water	½ cup
	maraschino cherries

Mix butter and sugar until creamy. Add eggs. Dissolve baking soda in water; add to egg mixture. Add flour and spices and mix. Stir in nuts and fruits. Drop teaspoon-sized hunks onto greased pan. Bake at 350° for 7 to 10 minutes.

FOUR DOZEN COOKIES

16 ounces candied fruit
½ cup
   all-purpose flour
¼ teaspoon salt

1 can coconut
2 cups chopped pecans
1 can sweetened
   condensed milk

Mix together fruit and flour. Stir in other ingredients, drop on greased cookie sheet and bake at 275° for 15 minutes.

The oil in pecans is about 95% and most of the oil is mono-unsaturated.

ORANGE COOKIES

1 pound vanilla wafers, finely crushed
1 box powdered sugar, sifted
1 cup chopped pecans
1 stick margarine, melted
6 ounces frozen orange juice
Coconut, optional
Powdered sugar, optional

Mix vanilla wafers, powdered sugar and pecans together. Add margarine and orange juice and roll into small balls. Roll in coconut or additional powdered sugar if desired. Cookies may be frozen.

MILLION DOLLAR COOKIES

2 cups butter or margarine	2 teaspoons baking powder
2 cups sugar	2 teaspoons baking soda
2 cups brown sugar	24 ounces chocolate chips
4 eggs	8 ounces Hershey bar, grated
2 teaspoons vanilla	3 cups chopped pecans
4 cups flour	
5 cups oatmeal flour*	
1 teaspoon salt	

Cream together margarine and sugars. Add eggs and vanilla. Mix togther flour, oat flour, salt, baking powder and baking soda; combine with butter mixture. Stir in remaining ingredients. Drop by golf ball size tablespoonfuls onto ungreased cookie sheet. Bake at 375° for 15 minutes. Makes 112 cookies.

*Measure oatmeal first; put small amounts of oatmeal into blender and blend until fine.

CHOCOLATE DIPS

2½ cups sifted flour
¼ teaspoon salt
1 cup butter
½ cup sugar
3 egg yolks
1 teaspoon
  almond extract

6 ounces semi-sweet
  chocolate chips,
  melted
½ cup pecans,
  chopped fine

Sift flour and salt; set aside. Cream butter and sugar until fluffy. Add egg yolks and almond extract. Mix thoroughly. Add dry ingredients slowly, mixing well. Using a cookie press, form into bars about 2 inches long on ungreased baking sheets. Bake in preheated 400° oven about 7 minutes. Cool. Dip ends of cookies in melted chocolate and sprinkle with pecans. Yield: 8 dozen.

EASY BROWNIES

½ cup margarine   2 eggs
1 cup sugar   ½ cup sifted flour
7 tablespoons cocoa   1 cup pecans

Cream margarine and sugar; add cocoa, then eggs, one at a time. Beat well; add remaining ingredients. Bake in shallow buttered pan at 325° for 20 to 30 minutes.

DATE AND PECAN FINGERS

¼ teaspoon salt
3 egg whites
1¾ cups
  powdered sugar

1 tablespoon flour
2 cups broken pecans
1 cup chopped dates
1 teaspoon vanilla

Add salt to egg whites; beat until stiff. Add sugar, sifted with flour, one tablespoon at a time. Fold in nuts, dates and vanilla. Drop by teaspoonfuls onto greased cookie sheet and shape into fingers. Bake at 300° for 30 minutes. Yields 3 dozen.

OLD RANGER COOKIES

½ cup butter
½ cup white sugar
½ cup brown sugar
1 egg, well beaten
1 cup flour, sifted
½ teaspoon soda
½ teaspoon
  baking powder

½ teaspoon vanilla
Pinch salt
¼ cup coconut
1 cup oatmeal
½ cup Rice Krispies
½ cup pecans
½ cup raisins

Cream first 3 ingredients. Add egg and mix well. Add remaining ingredients and drop from spoon onto greased cookie sheet. Bake at 350° for 12 to 15 minutes.

SHAKER CHOCOLATE CHIP COOKIES

2 sticks margarine
1½ cups brown sugar
2 eggs
1 teaspoon soda

1 teaspoon vanilla
2¼ cups
   self-rising flour*
8 ounces chocolate chips
1 cup chopped pecans

Turn oven to 350° and place margarine on cookie sheet in oven to melt. Mix together sugar and eggs; add soda, vanilla and melted margarine. Stir in flour, ½ at a time. Add chocolate chips and pecans and stir. Spread entire batter onto cookie sheet and bake for 10 to 12 minutes. Cut in squares and serve.

*You may wish to substitute ½ of this with oatmeal, raisin bran cereal, or whatever feels healthy.

DESSERTS

FRUIT COCKTAIL CAKE

2 cups flour
1¾ cups sugar
2 eggs

2 teaspoons soda
Pinch salt
1 can fruit cocktail

Icing:
1 small can coconut
1 stick margarine,
  melted

1 small can
  evaporated milk
¾ sup sugar
1 teaspoon vanilla
1 cup pecans

Beat eggs, add sugar and dry ingredients. Stir in
fruit cocktail. Bake in 9 x 13 x 2 pan at 350° for 30
minutes. Prepare icing by stirring all ingredients
except pecans together. Cook 5 minutes; add nuts
and spread on cake.

ICE BOX FRUIT CAKE

1 tall can
 evaporated milk
16 ounces
 marshmallows
16 ounces vanilla
 wafers, crushed
16 ounces raisins
8 ounces crystallized
 cherries, chopped

8 ounces crystallized
 pineapple, chopped
1 jar maraschino
 cherries, drained
4 cups chopped pecans
16 ounces coconut,
 optional

Heat milk in top of double boiler; add
marshmallows, stirring until melted. Remove
from heat and let cool. Mix remaining ingredients
and add cooled mixture. Pack in boxes. Makes
exact amount to fit in two 16-ounce vanilla
wafer boxes. Keep refrigerated. Unwrap and
slice.

TURTLE CAKE

1 box German
  chocolate cake mix
½ cup
  melted margarine
1 can sweetened
  condensed milk,
  divided

12 ounces
  chocolate chips
14 ounces caramels
½ cup milk
1 cup chopped pecans

Mix cake as directed, adding before mixing the melted margarine and ½ can condensed milk. Pour half of batter into greased and floured 9 x 13 x 2 inch pan and bake at 350° for 15 minutes. Meanwhile, melt caramels and chocolate chips with milk and remainder of condensed milk in double boiler. Add pecans and pour over cake while hot and top with remainder of batter. Return to oven for 30 minutes and sift confectioner's sugar over cooled cake.

HOT FUDGE PUDDING CAKE

1 cup flour
¾ cup sugar
2 tablespoons cocoa
2 teaspoons
  baking powder
¼ teaspoon salt
½ cup milk

2 tablespoons
  shortening, melted
1 cup chopped pecans
1 cup brown sugar,
  packed
¼ cup cocoa
1¾ cups hot water

Mix first 5 ingredients. Stir in milk, shortening and nuts. Pour batter into ungreased 9 x 9 x 2 baking pan. Combine brown sugar and cocoa. Sprinkle over batter in pan. Pour hot water over batter. Do not stir. Bake at 350° for 45 minutes. While hot, cut pudding into squares, invert onto dessert dishes and spoon sauce over each. Serve warm, topped with whipped cream or ice cream. Serves 9.

HARVEST LOAF CAKE

1¾ cups flour
1 teaspoon soda
½ teaspoon salt
1 teaspoon cinnamon
½ teaspoon nutmeg
¼ teaspoon ginger
¼ teaspoon
   ground cloves

½ cup butter
1 cup sugar
2 eggs
¾ cup
   canned pumpkin
¾ cup chocolate chips
¾ cup pecans

Grease loaf pans. Combine flour, soda, salt and spices. Cream butter, gradually add sugar and cream well. Blend in eggs; beat well. Add dry ingredients, blending alternately with pumpkin. Stir in chocolate chips and ½ cup pecans. Pour into loaf pan and sprinkle with remaining pecans. Bake at 350° for 65 to 75 minutes. Cool. Drizzle with Spice Glaze.

Spice Glaze:
½ cup sifted
confectioner's sugar
⅛ teaspoon nutmeg

⅛ teaspoon cinnamon
1 to 2 tablespoons milk

Mix all ingredients, adding just enough milk to form a smooth consistency.

PAT'S PRALINE CHEESECAKE

1½ pounds
  cream cheese
2 cups brown sugar

3 eggs
2 tablespoons flour
2 teaspoons vanilla
½ cup pecans

Crust:
1 cup graham
  cracker crumbs

3 tablespoons sugar
3 tablespoons butter

Combine cream cheese and brown sugar in mixer; when thoroughly mixed, add remaining ingredients. Pour into crust that has been pressed into a 10-inch springform pan. Bake at 350° for 35 minutes. Serves 12.

CRANBERRY-PECAN
UPSIDE-DOWN CAKE

1 ½ cups cranberries
½ cup chopped pecans
½ cup
   butterscotch topping
⅓ cup margarine
⅔ cup sugar

1 egg
½ teaspoon vanilla
1 cup flour
1 ½ teaspoons
   baking powder
½ teaspoon salt
½ cup milk

Arrange cranberries and pecans in the bottom of a greased 8-inch square pan. Pour topping over. Cream margarine and sugar until light and fluffy. Blend in egg and vanilla. Combine dry ingredients; add to creamed mixture alternately with milk, mixing well after each addition. Pour batter over topping mixture. Bake at 350° for 45 minutes, or until toothpick inserted comes out clean. Immediately invert onto serving platter. Serve warm, topped with whipped cream or ice cream.

CHERRY DUMP CAKE

2 sticks margarine
1 can cherry pie filling
1 can crushed
    pineapple, undrained
1 box yellow cake mix
½ cup pecans

Slice 1 stick margarine in bottom of 9 x 13 pan. Pour in cherry pie filling, top with crushed pineapple. Spread both evenly in pan. Top with dry cake mix. Top with remaining margarine and sprinkle with pecans. Bake at 350° approximately 30 minutes.

BANANA CAKE

2 cups sugar	3 cups all-purpose flour
⅔ cup shortening	6 tablespoons sour milk
2 eggs	2 teaspoons vanilla
½ teaspoon salt	1 cup chopped pecans
2 teaspoons soda	2 cups mashed bananas (about 6)
2 teaspoons baking powder	

Cream sugar and shortening. Add eggs and blend.
Stir in dry ingredients; add milk and vanilla. Stir
in nuts and bananas. Pour into a large greased
tube pan. Bake at 350° for 1½ hours.

Note: This cake stays moist really well.

ORANGE-DATE-NUT CAKE

½ cup butter
  or margarine
⅔ cup milk
1 cup sugar
2 cups flour
2 eggs

1 teaspoon soda
1 cup chopped pecans
1 tablespoon
  grated orange rind
1 package
  chopped dates

Glaze:
1½ cups sugar

¾ cup orange juice
1 teaspoon orange peel

Mix all cake ingredients together. Bake in a 9 x 13 pan at 350° for 30 minutes or until done. Prepare glaze by combining all ingredients, stirring until dissolved. Punch holes in cake while still hot and drizzle with glaze.

APPLE CAKE

2 cups sugar
1½ cups vegetable oil
2 large eggs
2½ cups
  self-rising flour

1 teaspoon cinnamon
1 teaspoon cloves
3 cups chopped apples
1 cup pecans

Combine all ingredients and bake at 350° for 1 hour.

Texans reportedly consume more pecans than anyone, but Georgia produces the most, and Louisiana may have been first to use them in its cookery, perhaps starting with the venerable and delicious praline.

BLUEBERRY CHEESE PIE

8 ounces cream cheese,
  softened
1 tablespoon
  heavy cream
1 teaspoon
  grated lemon rind

1 cup powdered sugar
⅛ teaspoon salt
3 eggs
1 cup blueberries
1 cup chopped pecans
1 large
  graham cracker crust

Glaze:
¼ cup
  granulated sugar
1½ tablespoons
  cornstarch

Dash salt
½ cup water
1 cup blueberries

In bowl, combine cheese, cream and lemon rind.
Add sugar, salt and eggs. Beat 5 minutes or until
smooth and creamy. Fold in berries. Cover crust
with chopped pecans. Pour cheese mix over nuts.
Bake at 350° for 30 minutes or until set. Allow to
stand until cold. Spoon glaze over pie. Refrigerate.

For glaze: mix sugar, cornstarch and salt in small
saucepan. Add water and berries. Bring to boil,
stirring. Cook slowly, stirring, about 5 minutes,
until clear and thick.

COOL WHIP FRUIT PIE

1 can sweetened
  condensed milk
⅓ cup lemon juice
1 cup chopped pecans
1 can fruit cocktail,
  drained
1 small can
  crushed pineapple

1 small bottle
  maraschino cherries,
  drained
1 teaspoon vanilla
1 large size Cool Whip
2 baked pie shells

Mix ingredients, adding Cool Whip last. Pour
into pie crusts. Refrigerate.

FROZEN WONDERFUL PIE

2 pie crusts
7 ounces coconut
1 cup chopped pecans
½ stick butter
8 ounces softened
  cream cheese

16 ounces non-dairy
  whipped topping
1 can sweetened
  condensed milk
Caramel ice cream
  topping

Brown pie crusts and set aside to cool. Using a skillet, brown coconut and pecans in butter. Set aside. Mix cream cheese, topping and milk until fluffy. Pour ½ topping mixture in pie crusts. Sprinkle ½ pecan mixture over topping. Drizzle caramel topping over top. Repeat. Wrap in plastic and freeze overnight. Will stay for 3 months in freezer.

GERMAN CHOCOLATE PIE

2 cups sugar
2 tablespoons flour
2 tablespoons cocoa
1 egg
1 tablespoon
  melted margarine

1 large can
  evaporated milk
1 cup coconut
¼ cup chopped pecans
Unbaked pie shell

Mix sugar, flour and cocoa together. Add egg and margarine. Beat until smooth. Add milk, coconut and pecans. Pour into pie shell. Bake at 350° for 45 minutes.

This recipe handed down from the Old S & W Cafeteria in Charlotte, N.C.

FLORIDA PIE

3 egg whites
½ teaspoon
   baking powder
1 cup sugar

1 cup chopped pecans
17 Ritz crackers,
   crushed
Cool Whip topping

Beat egg whites until foamy. Add baking powder and sugar, a small amount at a time; beat until stiff. Fold in pecans and cracker crumbs. Bake at 350° for 25 minutes. Cool and spread Cool Whip over pie. Recipe doubles well.

*T*here are numerous and conflicting claims regarding the origin of the pecan pie, but the most surprising note may be that practically no one baked it until the mid-1930s.

EXQUISITE PIE

3 eggs
1 cup sugar
1 stick margarine
  or butter
½ cup raisins

½ cup coconut
½ cup chopped pecans
1 tablespoon lemon
  juice or vinegar
1 unbaked pie shell

Cream eggs, sugar and butter. Stir in raisins, coconut and pecans. Mix well. Add lemon juice or vinegar. Pour into pie shell and bake at 350° for 30 to 35 minutes.

FRENCH COCONUT PIE

2 eggs
1 cup sugar
½ cup margarine,
   melted
1 teaspoon vinegar

1 teaspoon vanilla
1 cup coconut
½ to ¾ cup
   chopped pecans
Unbaked pie shell

Combine all ingredients and pour into pie shell.
Bake at 350° for 45 minutes.

*T*he basic ingredients in pecan pie filling—eggs, butter, brown or white sugar, corn or cane syrup—were used earlier in this century as the basis for confections called molasses pie and transparent pie. The addition of pecans, however, did not occur for decades.

MAPLE PECAN PIE

14 ounces sweetened
  condensed milk
½ cup maple syrup
2 tablespoons honey
1 cup ricotta cheese

1 tablespoon
  lemon juice
½ cup chopped pecans
1 teaspoon vanilla
Baked pie shell

Bring milk, syrup and honey to a boil over medium heat. Simmer, stirring until thickened. Remove from heat and add ricotta and lemon juice. Beat with an egg beater until mixture is smooth. Add pecans and vanilla and mix well. Pour into pie shell and refrigerate until completely cool. Serves 6 to 8.

PECAN MINIATURES

3 ounces cream cheese
1 stick margarine
1 cup flour
1 ½ cups light
  brown sugar

2 tablespoons
  margarine
2 eggs
2 teaspoons vanilla
1 ⅓ cups
  chopped pecans

Mix together cream cheese, margarine and flour for crust. Refrigerate 30 minutes. Cream brown sugar, margarine and eggs. Stir in vanilla and pecans. Line bottoms and sides of miniature muffin tins with small amounts of crust mixture. Fill with pecan mixture. Bake at 350° for 20 minutes. Makes 30 miniature tarts.

Mini-chocolate chips may be placed on top of crust before filling with pecan mixture for a special treat.

BROWN SUGAR PECAN PIE

1¼ cups pecan halves
1 unbaked pie shell
1½ cups brown sugar, packed
½ cup white sugar
⅛ teaspoon salt

2 tablespoons flour
2 or 3 eggs, lightly beaten
⅓ stick butter, melted
⅓ to ½ cup milk or light cream

Spread pecans over bottom of pie shell. Blend together all other ingredients, but do not overmix. Pour into shell. Bake at 350° for 30 to 40 minutes or until pie is light brown and set. (Pie is done when all but small circle in center is set. Heat from pie will make this firm after removing from oven.) This makes a large pie.

MAMA'S PECAN PIE

2 whole eggs	½ stick butter, melted
¾ cup sugar	1 teaspoon vinegar
2 tablespoons flour	1 teaspoon vanilla
½ cup white syrup	1 cup pecans
Dash salt	1 unbaked pie shell

Mix all together and bake 10 minutes at 425° and 30 minutes at 350° or until done.

PEACH-PECAN PIE

3 egg whites
1 cup sugar
12 soda crackers
(double)
¼ teaspoon
baking powder

1 teaspoon vanilla
½ cup crushed pecans
1 can sliced peaches,
drained
1 carton whipping
cream, whipped

Beat egg whites with sugar. Crush soda crackers until fine and add to beaten egg whites and sugar. Add baking powder and vanilla; beat well. Add crushed pecans and mix well. Pour into buttered pie plate and shape for pie shell. Bake at 350° for 30 minutes. Cool well. Pour drained peaches into shell, leaving 6 slices to put on top. Cover with whipped cream, arrange extra peach slices on top. Cool and refrigerate overnight before serving.

OZARK PUDDING

1 egg
¾ cup sugar
4 tablespoons
  all-purpose flour
1 teaspoon
  baking powder

⅛ teaspoon salt
2 cups grated
  unpeeled apples
½ cup pecans
Whipped cream

Beat together egg and sugar. Add flour, baking
powder and salt. Add apples and mix well; add
nuts and mix. Bake in a shallow greased pan at
300° for 30 minutes. Top with whipped cream.

PINEAPPLE PECAN PUDDING

20½ ounces
   pineapple tidbits
1½ cups packaged
   biscuit mix
½ cup chopped pecans

⅓ cup milk
½ cup brown sugar
2 tablespoons butter
   or margarine
Dash nutmeg
Dash cinnamon

Drain pineapple, reserving syrup. Combine biscuit mix, pineapple tidbits, and pecans. Stir in milk; spread in greased 10 x 6 x 1½ inch baking dish. Add water to pineapple syrup to make 1½ cups; combine with remaining ingredients in saucepan; bring to a boil. Pour evenly over batter. Bake at 350° for 35 to 40 minutes. Serve warm with whipped cream or ice cream.

APPLE CRISP

6 apples, pared,
  cored and sliced
1 cup sugar, divided
¼ teaspoon cloves
¼ teaspoon cinnamon
½ teaspoon nutmeg

2 tablespoons
  lemon juice
¾ cup flour, sifted
⅛ teaspoon salt
6 tablespoons butter
¼ cup chopped pecans

Preheat oven to 350°. Place apples in bowl; add ½ cup sugar, spices and lemon juice. Mix lightly, and place in buttered 11 x 7 x 2 baking dish. Blend remaining sugar, flour, salt, butter and pecans until crumbly. Sprinkle over apple mixture. Bake 45 minutes or until apples are tender and crust is browned. Serve warm or cold. Serves 6 to 8.

INDEX

DESSERTS